Katie and Her Butterfly Voice

Written and Illustrated by

Hana Carpenter

Butterfly House Books

Katie and Her Butterfly Voice
Written and Illustrated by Hana Carpenter

Copyright © 2026 by Hana Carpenter
All rights reserved.

No part of this book may be reproduced, distributed, or transmitted in any form or by any means, including photocopying, recording, or other electronic or mechanical methods, without the prior written permission of the publisher, except in the case of brief quotations embodied in critical reviews or certain other noncommercial uses permitted by copyright law.

Library of Congress Control Number: 2026900735

ISBN: 979-8-9935158-1-6 (hardback)

First Edition

Lansing, MI

Printed in the United States of America

Cover and Illustrations Copyright © 2026 by Hana Carpenter

Published by Butterfly House Books
www.butterflyhousebooks.com

About Butterfly House Books
Butterfly House Books is an independent publisher dedicated to creating stories that inspire children and families with messages of hope, resilience, and imagination. Founded in a home full of laughter, butterflies, and three little girls who never gave up, we tell stories that honor the soft, strong magic of growing into yourself.

For my daughters.

You make me brave.

And to my husband —
thank you for believing in me,
even on the days I doubted myself.

Katie was five years old,
with eyes like the sea
and hair like sunshine.

She loved to swing high
and climb even higher.
Her laugh swirled in the air
with the *butterflies*.

But sometimes,
when Katie was speaking,
the words didn't come out quite right.

Her brain and her mouth
had to work so hard
just to make the sounds
fit together.

That took a lot of practice!

Other kids could speak *fast*.

Their words seemed ready
as soon as they thought them.

For Katie, every word was a puzzle.
And she had to work hard
to put the sounds together.

Why is it so hard for me?"
she asked her mom.

Her mom pulled her into a hug.

*"Your brain works extra hard
to make your sounds.
That makes you strong!"*
she said.

*"You're learning to speak in ways
that are just as powerful,
even if they're different."*

Katie smiled.

She liked that.

Her big sister, Audrey, helped explain things when Katie couldn't find the words.

And Olive - even though she was small - seemed to understand Katie better than anyone.

"They get me," Katie thought.

"Even when I'm not saying much at all."

One day, Katie had an idea.
She wanted to explain a new game to her friends.

She used sticks to mark the path.
She showed them how to play with
movements and drawings.

Soon, everyone was laughing
and playing together.
"Your games are so much fun!"
Audrey said.

Katie's heart filled up.

Her way made room for everyone.

Katie still worked hard
to use her words.

Her speech therapist helped her
every week.

With Dad there,
she felt brave.

Katie didn't need to sound
like everyone else
to be heard.

Katie finds lots of ways to be heard.

Her voice helps people to listen with their eyes and their hearts.

Katie's voice is in her *smile*.

In her *drawings*.

In her *eyes*,
when they light up with ideas.

And even when
her words **wobble**.

her heart speaks loud and clear.

The end.

But just the beginning for Katie.

Author's Note

When my daughter was diagnosed with childhood apraxia of speech, I remember how helpless I felt. I watched her struggle to be understood. I watched her give up and go quiet—not because she had nothing to say, but because it was so hard to get the words out.

I wrote this book because I couldn't find one that reflected our experience. I wanted my daughter to see a character like her—someone who reminded her that her voice matters, even if it sounds different. I wanted other parents to know: it's going to be okay.

If you are holding this book and standing where I once stood, I want you to know your child's voice is powerful. Communication comes in many forms. And there is so much hope ahead.

With love,

Hana

WANT TO LEARN MORE ABOUT APRAXIA?

Apraxia Kids — www.apraxia-kids.org

Child Apraxia Treatment — www.childapraxiatreatment.org

ASHA (American Speech-Language-Hearing Association) — www.asha.org

Support & Connection — Online groups and local organizations exist for families navigating apraxia, offering encouragement and shared experiences. A speech-language pathologist can suggest games, activities, and tools that make communication practice easier and more fun. Communication can happen in many ways—through gestures, signs, pictures, or sounds—and each way is meaningful.

ABOUT BUTTERFLY HOUSE BOOKS

- where stories take flight -

Butterfly House Books was born in a home full of love, imagination, and the kind of strength that doesn't back down. Inspired by three unstoppable girls, we create stories that celebrate difference, resilience, and the many bright ways children shine.

Visit us at www.ButterflyHouseBooks.com to learn more, find resources, or say hello.

For the children who work quietly, imagine endlessly, and one day show the world how far they can go.